I Can Use The Bathroom

Written by Chemise Taylor

Illustrated by Alexis B. Taylor

Copyright © 2019 by My Skills Books

Published by My Skills Books

All rights reserved. No part of this publication may be reproduced, distributed, or transmitted in any form or by any means, including photocopying, recording, or other electronic or mechanical methods, without the prior written permission of the publisher, except in the case of brief quotations embodied in critical reviews and certain other noncommercial uses permitted by copyright law.

First Printing, 2019.

ISBN: 978-1-951573-01-0

www.myskillsbooks.com

I need to use the bathroom!

I sit on the toilet to pee or poop.

I use toilet tissue or wet wipes to wipe myself clean.

After I wipe myself, I flush the toilet.

If it is smelly in the bathroom, I spray an air freshener.

I go to the sink and turn on the faucet.

I wet my hands.

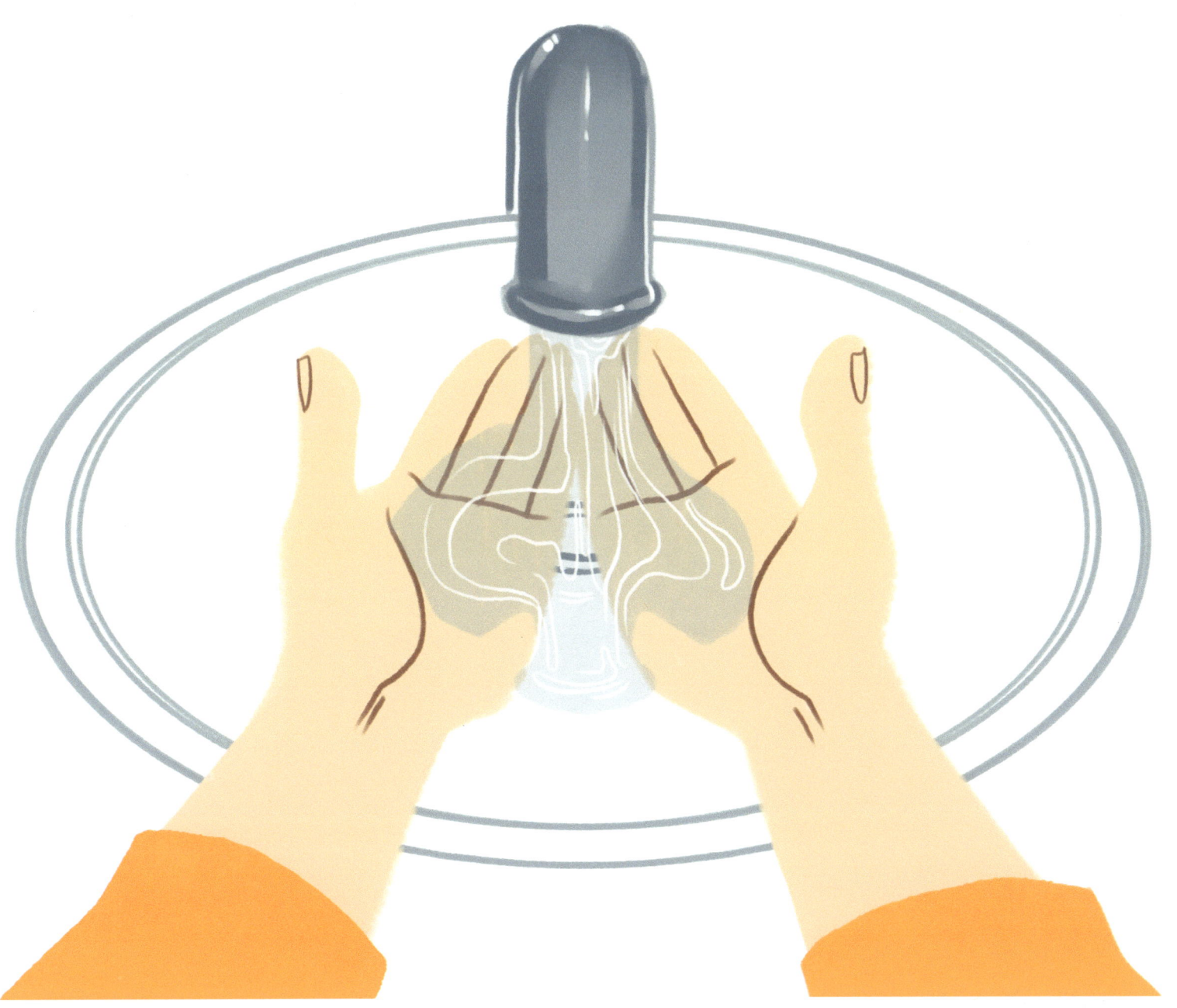

I lather the soap in my hands to get them nice and clean.

Then, I rinse my hands with water.

I dry the water from my hands with a towel.

Yay! I used the bathroom all by myself!

Book Details

Story Word Count: 106

Key Words: Flush, Wash, Toilet, Bathroom, Tissue, Wipe, Towel, Hands

Comprehension Check

- What was the story about?
- What does he sit on to pee or poop?
- What did he wipe himself with?

Reading Award

This certificate goes to:

_____

for reading "I Can Use The Bathroom"

Good Job!

More books, apps and resources at myskillsbooks.com

www.ingramcontent.com/pod-product-compliance
Lightning Source LLC
Chambersburg PA
CBHW042109090526
44591CB00004B/53